## SPOTLIGHT INTERACTIVE

# IN THE WILD

## ENCOUNTER SOME OF THE WORLD'S MOST EXOTIC ANIMALS

### BY JINNY JOHNSON

# CONTENTS

**Thunder Bay Press**

An imprint of the Advantage Publishers Group

10350 Barnes Canyon Road, San Diego, CA 92121

www.thunderbaybooks.com

All notations of errors or omissions should be addressed to Thunder Bay Press, Editorial Department, at the above address.

All other correspondence (author inquiries, permissions) concerning the content of this book should be addressed to The Book Studio Ltd, Garrard Way, Kettering, Northants NN16 8TD.

ISBN-13: 978-1-59223-955-9

ISBN-10: 1-59223-955-2

Printed in China.

1 2 3 4 5 12 11 10 09 08

# INTRODUCTION

Extinction is a natural part of life. Species come and go, and new ones take their places. One of the reasons our own group of animals, the mammals, became so successful was because of the death of the dinosaurs, which left opportunities open for the small mammals that already existed to diversify and fill many more niches.

But the difference now is that the rate of extinctions is speeding up like never before. There are thousands of animals and plants in danger of disappearing forever. Millions of years ago, there were several periods of mass extinctions when huge numbers of species disappeared. But these had natural causes, such as huge volcanic eruptions, meteorite impacts, and immense climate change. Now, human activity is destroying huge areas of natural habitat, such as rainforests and swampland. We have hunted animals out of existence, captured them as pets, disturbed their world by bringing in animals from other places, and persecuted them for parts of their bodies that we want—such as rhino and elephant horn. Pollution from chemicals and carelessly discarded waste harms countless animals every day.

Conservation organizations all over the world are working to protect habitats, set aside reserves for animals, breed young in captivity, and limit trade. Some of these measures will succeed but by no means all.

In this book we take a look at just some of the creatures that are already rare or becoming rare—animals such as elephants, rhinos, pandas, and polar bears—and it would be unimaginable to lose them. But there are other less familiar creatures that have an important role too—bats, insects, frogs, and lizards. The natural world is finely balanced and generally the loss of one creature has an impact on all those around it.

Conservationists have to be realistic. The world's population has increased enormously and people need homes and land to grow food. Somehow we need to balance human needs with those of the natural world and find ways that humans and animals can coexist.

## USING THIS BOOK

The animals shown here are only a tiny fraction of those in danger. Basic information is provided for each creature, together with an idea of its lifestyle and the particular problems that threaten its survival. Headings are as follows:

**Scientific name:** This name is in Latin and remains the same from country to country, whatever the language. The name describes some aspect of the animal or sometimes incorporates the name of the person who discovered it.

**Order/Family:** All animals are arranged into groups, which help clarify their relationships. For each animal in the book, we give the order and family to which it belongs. For example, one order of mammals is Carnivora, which includes a wide range of flesh-eating animals such as cats and dogs. The carnivore order is in turn divided into a number of different families, which share many characteristics: the cat family, dog family, bear family, and so on.

**Range:** The area in which the animal lives.

**Size:** The length, weight, or wingspan of the creature as appropriate.

**Conservation status:** The relative risk of extinction (see below).

## THREATENED SPECIES

One of the international organizations working with endangered species is the IUCN—the International Union for Conservation of Nature. They collate a vast amount of information to monitor the status of the world's wildlife. Each is given a category according to how serious the risk.

The most serious categories are as follows:
**Critically endangered:** extremely high risk of extinction in the wild
**Endangered:** a very high risk of extinction in the wild
**Vulnerable:** a high risk of extinction in the wild

**There are rare and endangered species in all groups of animals.**

## MAMMALS
Of the approximately 4,600 mammal species, more than 2,200 are currently on the IUCN's list of threatened species. Examples include the buffalo (Bubalus bubalis).

## REPTILES
Of the approximately 7,000 reptile species, more than 750 are currently on the IUCN's list of threatened species. Examples include the mugger crocodile (Crocodylus palustris).

## BIRDS
Of the nearly 10,000 bird species, more than 2,240 are currently on the IUCN's list of threatened species. Examples include Baer's pochard (Aythya baeri).

## AMPHIBIANS
Of the more than 5,000 amphibian species, more than 3,600 are currently on the IUCN's list of threatened species. Examples include the Mallorcan midwife toad (Alytes muletensis).

## INSECTS AND OTHER INVERTEBRATES
They may be more than 2 million species of invertebrate on Earth, but little is known about most of them. Around 1,000 insect species are already on the IUCN's list. Examples include the Queen Alexandra's birdwing butterfly (Ornithoptera alexandae).

## FISH
Of the approximately 25,000 fish species, more than 2,200 are currently on the IUCN's list of threatened species. Examples include the bala shark (Balantiocheilos melanopterus).

# GORILLAS

Gorillas are large, heavily built animals and the biggest of the primates (monkeys and apes). They belong to the same family of mammals as humans and are among our closest relatives.

## WESTERN GORILLA

**Scientific name:** Gorilla gorilla
**Order/Family:** Primates/Hominidae
**Range:** Central West Africa—Nigeria to Gabon and Congo
**Size:** Up to 6 ft. tall
**Conservation status:** Critically endangered

Western gorillas live in tropical forest, usually in family groups of up to 20 animals led by an adult male. The mature males are larger than females and can weigh twice as much. They are known as silverbacks because of the patch of silvery white hair that starts to appear on a male's back when he is around 15 years old. Fruit is the main food of Western gorillas. They are lighter and more agile than their Eastern relatives and so able to climb into trees more easily in search of food.

Gorillas are generally active during the day and start feeding soon after dawn. They rest in the middle of the day, then feed again in the late afternoon and early evening. At night they sleep in nests made of plant material. Infant gorillas sleep with their mothers.

### THREATS

The destruction of their forest home for farming and logging is one reason why Western gorillas are now rare. But many are also killed for their meat, known as bushmeat, which unfortunately is much in demand. Large numbers of gorillas have died from the Ebola virus, one of the most deadly viruses known.

# EASTERN GORILLA

**Scientific name:** Gorilla beringei
**Order/Family:** Primates/Hominidae
**Range:** Central Africa
**Size:** Up to 6 ft. 3 in. tall
**Conservation status:** Endangered

These gorillas are slightly larger than the Western gorillas and have longer faces and broader chests. There are two groups of Eastern gorilla—the lowland gorilla and the mountain gorilla, which lives in the Virunga volcano range in central Africa. Eastern gorillas have darker fur than Western gorillas and the mountain gorilla has particularly long hair to help keep it warm in its cool mountain home. Eastern gorillas feed mostly on leaves and do not usually travel so far to find food as their Western relatives. They live in family groups of 30 or more animals.

Female gorillas usually give birth to just one young, occasionally twins, every three or four years. The young are as helpless as a human baby at birth and are not weaned until they are over three years old. This low birth rate is one reason why gorilla numbers are low. The young animals learn their life skills from the other adults in the family group as well as from their parents.

A family of mountain gorillas.

A female mountain gorilla and her three-year-old young.

## THREATS

Poachers are a particular problem for mountain gorillas. And their popularity with tourists has also led to the animals catching human diseases to which they have no resistance. Other threats include war and unrest in their home region and traps set to catch other animals that can kill and injure gorillas and their young.

## •IN THE FIELD•

Gorillas are a protected species. A new United Nations project called The Great Apes Survival Project (GRASP) has been set up to help protect not only gorillas but also chimpanzees and orangutans. One important aim is to balance the needs of the great apes with those of people in the area and involve locals in the efforts to save the apes.

# CHIMPS AND ORANGUTANS

These animals are great apes like the gorillas. All are becoming increasingly rare in the wild and it is vital to continue conservation measures if they are to survive.

## CHIMPANZEE

**Scientific name:** Pan troglodytes
**Order/Family:** Primates/Hominidae
**Range:** Parts of equatorial Africa, particularly Gabon and Congo
**Size:** Head and body: up to 37 in. long
**Conservation status:** Endangered

Chimpanzees are strong, agile animals with longer arms than legs. Their long arms help them move easily in the trees. On the ground they usually walk on all fours but they can stand and walk upright for short periods. They live in family groups led by adult males.

Fruit and leaves are the chimpanzee's main foods, but it also eats insects, eggs, honey, and occasionally small mammals. Chimpanzees have been seen using tools such as sticks to reach honey or insects, or stones to crack nuts. Generally active during the day, chimpanzees sleep at night in nests made in the trees.

### THREATS

The main threats to chimpanzees are habitat loss, hunting for their meat, and the capture of young animals which often means shooting the mother. This is now illegal, but poaching of young for the live animal trade does still go on.

### •IN THE FIELD•

WWF and GRASP (Great Apes Survival Project) are working to establish reserves and links between reserves, and encouraging local people to protect apes. The Bonobo Conservation Initiative is dedicated to helping the bonobo and enforcing laws against hunting these animals. Several organizations are struggling to preserve areas of orangutan rainforest habitat.

# BONOBO

**Scientific name:** Pan paniscus
**Order/Family:** Primates/Hominidae
**Range:** Central Africa—Democratic Republic of Congo
**Size:** Head and body: up to 32 in. long
**Conservation status:** Endangered

### THREATS
Like chimpanzees, bonobos have suffered from the loss of their habitat as land is cleared for forestry and agriculture. But perhaps the greatest problem is the killing of animals for bushmeat.

Bonobos were the last apes to be discovered and were not known by scientists until 1933. They are also called pygmy chimpanzees, but in fact they are much the same length as the chimpanzee but with a more slender shape. Bonobos spend most of their time up in the trees feeding on fruit, leaves, and plant stems. They will sometimes eat small animals, but they do not seem to go on hunting raids like chimpanzees do. Bonobos are generally less aggressive than chimpanzees, and females have equal rank with males.

# BORNEAN ORANGUTAN

**Scientific name:** Pongo pygmaeus
**Order/Family:** Primates/Hominidae
**Range:** Borneo
**Size:** Head and body: up to 38 in. long
**Conservation status:** Endangered

The name orangutan means "person of the forest" and these apes are the largest tree-living animals in the world. They have very long arms, which help them swing from branch to branch, and shaggy reddish hair. Males are larger than females and develop large flaps at each side of the face. Unlike chimps and gorillas, orangutans generally live alone, except for mothers with young. Fruit is their main food, but they will eat leaves and seeds.

### THREATS
Like its cousins in Africa, the orangutan has suffered from loss of its rainforest habitat. It is thought that as much as 80 percent of the forest has been destroyed in the last 20 years. A particular problem has been the clearing of land for palm-oil plantations. Serious fires in recent years have also killed many.

# LEMURS AND MONKEYS

There are two main groups of monkeys—Old World monkeys and and New World monkeys. The New World monkeys include tamarins, marmosets, and howlers. Old World monkeys include baboons and macaques. Lemurs belong to a group of primates called prosimians.

## INDRI

**Scientific name:** Indri indri
**Order/Family:** Primates/Indridae
**Range:** Madagascar
**Size:** Head and body: up to 28 in. long; tail: up to 2 in.
**Conservation status:** Endangered

The largest of the lemurs, the indri spends most of its life in the trees, and fruit and leaves are its main foods. When on the ground, the indri cannot move around on all fours but stands upright and walks on its back legs. It lives in small family groups led by a female.

### THREATS

Indris are one of the most endangered of the lemurs. Much of their forest home has been destroyed. The population of Madagascar is increasing and many people have to rely on slash-and-burn agriculture to grow basic food supplies. To add to the problems the indri breeds slowly, producing young only every three years.

## •IN THE FIELD•

The indri does not breed well in captivity so its survival depends on enough of its habitat being preserved. In Brazil people now prize the golden lion tamarin and see it as a national symbol of conservation. Life is much harder for the proboscis monkey, which does not react well to life in captivity as it can only eat leaves and other plant food that grow in its native home.

# GOLDEN LION TAMARIN

**Scientific name:** Leontopithecus rosalia
**Order/Family:** Primates/Callitrichidae
**Range:** Southeast Brazil
**Size:** Head and body: up to 13 in. long; tail: up to 16 in.
**Conservation status:** Endangered

The beautiful little tamarin monkey with its silky golden fur is a conservation success story. In 1996 and 2000 it was critically endangered but its population has increased and it is now listed as endangered. It spends most of its life in the trees eating a wide range of foods such as fruit, insects, eggs, and small animals.

## THREATS
Much of the tamarin's forest habitat has been destroyed and many were captured for zoos and for sale as pets, but this is illegal. Tamarins bred in captivity have been reintroduced into the wild and have now bred so their numbers are increasing.

# PROBOSCIS MONKEY

**Scientific name:** Nasalis larvatus
**Order/Family:** Primates/Cercopithecidae
**Range:** Borneo
**Size:** Head and body: up to 30 in. long; tail: up to 29 in.
**Conservation status:** Endangered

The male proboscis monkey is much larger than the female and has a very big fleshy nose. No one knows quite why the monkey has a nose like this but it may help him attract mates as it also enables him to make a loud honking sound. The monkeys have big potbellies because they have special compartments in their stomach to help them digest their diet of tough leaves.

## THREATS
Huge areas of Borneo forest have been cleared for timber and for growing oil palms. The proboscis monkey is very sensitive to disturbance and needs large areas of forest if it is to find enough to eat. Many monkeys have been shot by hunters, although hunting is now illegal.

# PANDAS AND OTHER BEARS

There are eight different kinds of bear, including the giant panda. Most are becoming increasingly rare but there are still fairly large numbers of brown bears and American black bears.

## GIANT PANDA

**Scientific name:** Ailuropoda melanoleuca
**Order/Family:** Carnivora/Ursidae
**Range:** Southwest China
**Size:** Head and body: up to 5 ft. long; tail: 5 in.
**Conservation status:** Endangered

Pandas are large, heavily built animals with distinctive black and white markings. They live in mountain forest areas and feed almost entirely on bamboo. There isn't much goodness in bamboo so pandas have to eat 45 lb or more a day to get enough nourishment. Females give birth to one cub that is small and poorly developed at birth. The cub stays with its mother for two years or more, but generally pandas live alone.

### THREATS

Loss of habitat has been the greatest problem for the panda. Large areas of bamboo forest have been cut down for agriculture and logging and now only small areas remain. Hunting pandas is illegal but some are still shot for their skins or caught in traps left for other animals.

A giant panda in the Wolong Reserve in Sichuan, China.

### •IN THE FIELD•

The survival of the giant panda depends on reserves that have been set up to protect its bamboo forest home. Around two-thirds of wild pandas, probably about 1,000 animals, live in these reserves. The WWF is now working on creating "corridors" of bamboo forest between the reserves so the animals can move more easily from area to area.

# ASIATIC BLACK BEAR

**Scientific name:** Ursus thibetanus
**Order/Family:** Carnivora/Ursidae
**Range:** Central and eastern Asia
**Size:** Head and body: up to 6 ft. long; tail: 4 in.
**Conservation status:** Vulnerable

A bulky, shaggy animal, this bear has a creamy, crescent-shaped marking on its chest. It eats nuts, fruits, and berries. It climbs well and spends much of its time in trees. The female usually gives birth to two cubs in a safe den in a hollow tree. The cubs stay with her for up to 18 months.

### THREATS
Asiatic black bears have long been hunted for their gall bladders and bile, which is used in traditional Chinese medicine. Bears are also killed for their skin and their paws, considered a luxury food. Hunting is now illegal in most countries except Japan, but poaching continues.

# POLAR BEAR

**Scientific name:** Ursus maritimus
**Order/Family:** Carnivora/Ursidae
**Range:** Northern North America, Greenland, northern Eurasia
**Size:** Head and body: up to 8 ft. long; tail: 5 in.
**Conservation status:** Vulnerable

The polar bear is the largest of all land carnivores. It is well adapted for its Arctic home with a coat of thick white fur, which covers its whole body except for the soles of its feet and its nose. An expert hunter, it feeds mostly on seals, but also catches walruses, small whales, and birds. It swims well and has big forepaws that act as paddles. Females give birth to two or three cubs, which stay with them for more than two years.

### THREATS
There are reasonable numbers of polar bears at present, but this could all change with global warming. As areas of sea ice get smaller it is harder for the bears to find enough food to survive. Pollutants, particularly in the fatty blubber of their prey, are also affecting the well being of the polar bears. Hunting of the bears by local people is allowed to provide meat and fur.

# BIG CATS

The largest members of the cat family are some of the most magnificent of all animals. Yet they are now increasingly rare and are suffering from loss of large areas of their habitat and fewer prey animals.

## TIGER

**Scientific name:** Panthera tigris
**Order/Family:** Carnivora/Felidae
**Range:** Asia—Siberia to India and Southeast Asia
**Size:** Head and body: up to 9 ft. long; tail: up to 43 in.
**Conservation status:** Endangered

The magnificent tiger is the biggest of the big cats. Its stripy coat is instantly recognizable and, amazingly, each tiger has a slightly different stripe pattern. There were once eight subspecies of tiger, living in parts of Asia from Siberia in the far north to Sumatra in Southeast Asia. India now has the largest numbers of tigers, but all are rare and the Caspian, Javan, and Bali tigers are extinct.

Most tigers live in forested areas, but some are found in grassland and swamps. They generally hunt at night, preying on creatures such as deer, wild pigs, and buffalo

### THREATS
Tigers were once shot for "sport" and this began their decline. Hunting is now illegal but much of their forest habitat has been destroyed. Tigers are still shot by farmers to protect livestock and many are poached for their body parts, which are used in Chinese medicine. This trade is illegal but still goes on because the financial rewards are high.

A tiger carrying its prey.

### •IN THE FIELD•
Some successful tiger reserves have been set up, particularly in India. Conservation organizations such as WWF and IUCN are trying to involve local people in their efforts and attempting to control the trade in body parts for use in traditional Chinese medicine.

# SNOW LEOPARD

**Scientific name:** Uncia uncia
**Order/Family:** Carnivora/Felidae
**Range:** Central Asia
**Size:** Head and body: up to 4 ft. 4 in.; tail: up to 39 in.
**Conservation status:** Endangered

The snow leopard is rarely seen in the wild. It lives high in the rugged mountains of Central Asia and is usually active at night or at dawn and dusk. Its smoky gray fur is extremely thick and it has a dense undercoat for added insulation. Wild sheep and goats, deer, and young yak are the snow leopard's main prey, but it will also hunt livestock if prey is scarce.

## THREATS

There are probably between 5,000 and 7,500 snow leopards left in the wild. The fur trade threat has declined now but snow leopards are still killed by poachers and their skins sold. Increasingly these cats are hunted instead of tigers for their body parts for use in traditional Chinese medicine.

# LION

**Scientific name:** Panthera leo
**Order/Family:** Carnivora/Felidae
**Range:** Africa, south of the Sahara; Gir Forest in India
**Size:** Head and body: up to 8 ft. 3 in. long; tail: 39 in.
**Conservation status:** Vulnerable

## THREATS

Many lions used to be shot for "sport," but this is now allowed in only a few African countries. Some are still killed because of attacks on livestock. An increase in agricultural land has also reduced the lion's habitat and numbers of its prey animals. Fortunately for the lion, people are now realizing its value as a tourist attraction and that will help to safeguard its future.

The largest carnivores in Africa, lions live mainly in savanna areas and open woodland. They are the most social of the cats and live in groups of several adult animals and their cubs. They hunt together, too, and attack much larger animals, such as wildebeest and zebra. Lions are not yet as rare as tigers, at least in Africa, but numbers of Asian lions are very low and there are probably only about 300, all in the Gir Forest reserve in India.

# CHEETAHS AND OTHER CATS

Cheetahs and other cats such as the lynx are smaller than lions and tigers, but still expert hunters. Like their larger relatives, many have been hunted for their beautiful fur.

## CHEETAH

**Scientific name:** Acinonyx jubatus
**Order/Family:** Carnivora/Felidae
**Range:** Africa, south of the Sahara
**Size:** Head and body: up to 5 ft. long; tail: 31 in.
**Conservation status:** Vulnerable

The cheetah is the world's fastest land animal and can sprint at up to 70 miles an hour for short distances. With its flexible spine and its long legs and tail, the cheetah is built for speed, and it preys on other fast runners such as gazelle and impalas. It hunts by getting as close as possible to its prey and then making a final high-speed chase. Unlike other cats, the cheetah cannot pull in its claws—they help it keep its grip as it runs. Cheetahs do not roar like lions and tigers. Instead they purr, growl, and make a chirping sound.

## THREATS
Loss of prey caused by hunting by humans is a problem for cheetahs and they themselves are shot if they go near livestock. In wildlife reserves cheetahs suffer from competition with lions and hyenas, both of which may steal cheetahs' kills. Lions and hyenas also kill cheetah cubs if they come across them.

# AFRICAN GOLDEN CAT

**Scientific name:** Profelis aurata
**Order/Family:** Carnivora/Felidae
**Range:** West and central Africa
**Size:** Head and body: up to 3 ft. long; tail: 18 in.
**Conservation status:** Vulnerable

The African golden cat lives in the rainforest and is rarely seen. Like most cats, it lives and hunts alone, taking prey such as rats and other small mammals and birds. It also sometimes preys on larger domestic animals such as sheep and goats. Although it generally hunts on the ground, the African golden cat is also a good climber.

## THREATS

Like other rainforest animals, the golden cat has been badly affected by the loss of large areas of its habitat. Fortunately, though, it does have a wide range of prey and seems to be able to survive on creatures such as rats, which are plentiful even in disturbed forest. Although in most countries in its range it is illegal to hunt this cat, poaching does still go on and skins are sold in markets. Farmers also kill golden cats that prey on livestock or attack poultry.

# IBERIAN LYNX

**Scientific name:** Lynx pardinus
**Order/Family:** Felidae
**Range:** Spain and Portugal
**Size:** Head and body: up to 3 ft. 6 in. long; tail 12 in.
**Conservation status:** Critically endangered

here are probably fewer than 1,000 Iberian lynx ʒft in the wild. Numbers declined in the 1950s fter myxomatosis destroyed large numbers of ɪbbits—their main prey.

ɪhis animal is in greater danger of becoming xtinct than any other wild cat. Like a larger ʒersion of a domestic cat, the lynx has pale spotted ɪr, big tufted ears, and a ruff of fur on its cheeks.

xpert hunters, these cats live in forests, woodland, ɪnd scrub, and prey on creatures such as rabbits ɪnd birds. They generally hunt at night and are ɔlitary animals. Females give birth to one to four ɔung in spring.

## THREATS

Lynx have suffered from loss of habitat as large areas of scrub and woodland have been cleared for agriculture and industry. Hunting lynx is illegal but still goes on, and many animals are also caught in traps left for other animals or killed by poisoned fox bait.

# WOLVES AND WILD DOGS

The dog family include animals such as wolves and foxes as well as several kinds of wild dog. Many, such as the gray wolf and the red fox, are still common but a few species are becoming rare, partly due to hunting by humans.

## RED WOLF

**Scientific name:** Canis rufus
**Order/Family:** Carnivora/Canidae
**Range:** Eastern United States
**Size:** Head and body: up to 4 ft.; tail: 12-15 in.
**Conservation status:** Critically endangered

Once widespread in the southern United States, the red wolf is now one of the rarest members of the dog family. It lives in forested areas and wetlands and hunts prey such as rabbits, raccoons, and deer. It lives in family groups consisting of a mated pair and their young.

### THREATS
Large numbers of these wolves used to be shot and trapped because farmers believed they killed livestock. The wolves also suffered from habitat loss as woodlands were cut down for farmland. The red wolf actually became extinct in the wild in 1980 when the remaining wild animals were captured to start a breeding program.

### •IN THE FIELD•
The saving of the red wolf has been a conservation success story. Following a captive breeding program with the last of the wild red wolves, four pairs were released into the wild in 1987. Now there are at least 100 red wolves living wild in North Carolina and there are another 150 or more in captivity breeding more animals for release.

# AFRICAN HUNTING DOG

**Scientific name:** Lycaon pictus
**Order/Family:** Carnivora/Canidae
**Range:** Parts of southern and eastern Africa
**Size:** Head and body: up to 3 ft. 6 in. long; tail: up to 16 in.
**Conservation status:** Endangered

## THREATS

Hunting dogs used to be very common in Africa south of the Sahara, but now there are only scattered packs. Their numbers are low partly because of loss of habitat and fewer prey animals, but also because so many have been shot and trapped. Diseases such as rabies and distemper, which the wild dogs catch from domestic dogs, have also killed large numbers. There are now probably only 5,000 or so of these hunting dogs left in the wild.

These wild dogs live in close-knit groups led by a dominant male and female pair. They hunt as a pack and work together to bring down animals much larger than themselves, such as wildebeest and zebra. They can run fast and keep going for long distances.

A pack of African hunting dogs feeding on their prey.

# DHOLE

**Scientific name:** Cuon alpinus
**Order/Family:** Carnivora/Canidae
**Range:** Southern Asia
**Size:** Head and body up to 3 ft. 6 in. long; tail: up to 20 in.
**Conservation status:** Endangered

Also known as the Asiatic wild dog, the dhole lives in packs of about 10 animals. The dogs usually hunt together too, particularly in the breeding season when food has to be supplied to young cubs, and they can bring down large deer and cattle such as the banteng. The dhole has an unusual whistle-like call that it uses to keep in touch with others in the pack.

## THREATS

The needs of the ever-increasing population in the dhole's range has led to much of their habitat being cleared for farmland and timber. In the past, many dhole have been shot by hunters, but they are now protected in most countries. In fact, the biggest dhole packs live in tiger reserves in India.

# WHALES AND DOLPHINS

Although they spend all their lives in the water, whales and dolphins are mammals and have to come to the surface to breathe. Many are now rare due to hunting and to damage by pollution and fishing nets.

## BLUE WHALE

**Scientific name:** Balaenoptera musculus
**Order/Family:** Cetacea/Balaenopteridae
**Range:** All oceans
**Size:** Up to 100 ft. long; weight: over 100 tons
**Conservation status:** Endangered

The blue whale is the largest animal that has ever lived, bigger even than the dinosaurs. Despite its huge size, it feeds entirely on tiny shrimplike creatures called krill and it may eat as much as 4 tons of these a day. It filters its food from the water through special fringed structures in its mouth called baleen plates. Most whales spend the summer months in cool or temperate waters near the North or South Pole. In winter they migrate to warmer waters nearer the equator where they mate and give birth to their young.

### THREATS

In the first half of the twentieth century, thousands of blue whales were killed for the oil from their blubber. Now whales are hunted more for their meat, but in 1966 all killing of blue whales was banned. However, some illegal hunting continues and, although numbers have been slowly increasing, these whales are still very rare.

### •IN THE FIELD•

Whales and dolphins are protected when areas of ocean are set aside, safe from whale hunters. The Southern Ocean and Indian Ocean whale sanctuaries have banned all commercial whaling. In New Zealand, the Marine Mammals Protection Act has made it illegal to kill or injure any marine mammal. Two marine mammal sanctuaries are established around the coasts of New Zealand.

# HUMPBACK WHALE

**Scientific name:** Megaptera novaeangliae
**Order/Family:** Cetacea/Balaenopteridae
**Range:** All oceans
**Size:** Up to 50 ft. long; weight: 33 tons
**Conservation status:** Vulnerable

The humpback is an amazingly acrobatic whale. It often leaps up out of the water or lifts its huge flippers or tail and slaps the water surface. The flippers are up to 16 ft. long with lots of knobs and bumps at the front edge. Shrimplike krill and small fish are the humpback's main food. Male humpbacks sing long and complex "songs" which may help them attract females.

## THREATS
Since 1966 humpbacks have been protected from whalers but some are still taken. Humpbacks can also be injured by fishing equipment and pollution in the ocean, but numbers do seem to be increasing.

The balloon of spray created as a humpback breathes out.

# HECTOR'S DOLPHIN

**Scientific name:** Cephalorhynchus hectori
**Order/Family:** Cetacea/Delphinidae
**Range:** Pacific Ocean, coasts of New Zealand
**Size:** Up to 4 ft. 6 in. long; weight: up to 110 lb.
**Conservation status:** Endangered

Hector's dolphin is the smallest and rarest member of the dolphin family. Like all dolphins, it is a sociable animal and lives and feeds in groups. It eats fish, squid, and some shellfish. The clicking sounds it makes are called echolocation and help it find its prey, rather like seeing with sound.

## THREATS
These dolphins spend most of their time in coastal waters so are sometimes injured by boats and ships, and by pollution. Polluted waters can make the dolphins ill and they can choke on rubbish they swallow accidentally. But one of the worst problems is the danger of getting tangled in fishing nets. A dolphin is a mammal, and if it gets trapped and can't get to the surface to breathe, it will drown.

# SEALS, SEA LIONS, AND MANATEES

Like whales and dolphins, seals, sea lions, and manatees are all mammals even though they live in the sea.

## STELLER SEA LION

**Scientific name:** Eumetopias jubatus
**Order/Family:** Carnivora/Otariidae
**Range:** Northern Pacific coasts
**Size:** Up to 10 ft. long; weight: up to 1,500 lb. (males)
**Conservation status:** Endangered

Also known as the northern sea lion, this is the largest of the sea lions or eared seals. Males are twice the size of females. Steller sea lions are noisy, sociable animals, which gather in huge groups. They spend much of their time at sea, feeding on fish and squid, but they come to land to mate and give birth. Sea lions can move faster and more easily on land than seals, as they can tuck their back flippers under the body and use them to push themselves along.

### THREATS

Numbers of these seals have dropped by two-thirds over the last 20 years or so and no one quite knows why. Reasons could include pollution and disease as well as the dangers of fishing nets and predation by killer whales. Research is being carried out to try and find out exactly what has happened in order to protect the sea lions in the future.

A Steller sea lion caught in plastic waste.

### •IN THE FIELD•

Increasing levels of garbage in the ocean and in rivers are causing harm to many water-living animals. They may be made ill by poisonous substances, swallow plastic items that damage their insides or choke them, or get tangled in debris. Conservation organizations are trying to increase our awareness of these problems. Meanwhile everyone can help just a little by taking garbage home and not throwing it in the water or leaving it on beaches.

# AMERICAN MANATEE

**Scientific name:** Trichechus manatus
**Order/Family:** Sirenia/Trichechidae
**Range:** United States, Caribbean, and northeast South America
**Size:** Up to 13 ft. long; weight: up to 3,300 lb.
**Conservation status:** Vulnerable

A large mammal with a bulky body, paddlelike tail, and two flippers, the manatee spends all its life in water. Some manatees live in rivers, canals, and estuaries, while others stay in coastal waters. This gentle, slow-moving creature feeds entirely on plants, such as seagrass, and is sometimes known as the "sea cow." Females give birth to one young, occasionally twins, every two to five years.

## THREATS

Manatees were hunted for their meat and skin in the past but now the main threat is from injury by collisions with speedboats. Many animals also suffer from accidentally swallowing garbage or fish hooks or getting trapped in fishing lines. Conservation measures include better controls over boat speeds and the setting up of sanctuaries for these animals.

# HAWAIIAN MONK SEAL

**Scientific name:** Monachus schauinslandi
**Order/Family:** Carnivora/Phocidae
**Range:** Coastal waters, Hawaiian Islands
**Size:** Up to 7 ft. 6 in. long; weight: up to 450 lb.
**Conservation status:** Endangered

Most true seals live in cool waters but the Hawaiian monk seal stays in tropical seas all year round. It spends most of its time in the water, where it swims with the aid of its strong tail flippers, but it does come ashore to bask on beaches. It feeds on fish, squid, and other sea creatures.

## THREATS

Monk seals used to be hunted for their meat and skin and the oil from their blubber. They are no longer hunted but are at risk from the disturbance of their habitat by humans and, in some areas, from lack of prey. Many seals also get trapped in fishing nets or injured by debris floating in the water. Sharks also kill and eat these seals.

# OTTERS AND MINK

These animals all belong to the mustelid family, which also includes weasels and skunks.

## SEA OTTER

**Scientific name:** Enhydra lutris
**Order/Family:** Carnivora/Mustelidae
**Range:** Northern Pacific coasts
**Size:** Head and body: up to 4 ft. long; tail: up to 15 in.
**Conservation status:** Endangered

The smallest of the marine mammals, the sea otter is perfectly adapted for life in the sea, but also moves well on land. It has a slender, agile body, strong back feet that act as flippers for swimming, and a thick tail it uses as a rudder. Unlike seals, it does not have layers of fatty blubber to keep it warm. Instead it has the densest fur of any mammal—up to two million hairs per square inch. The sea otter is one of the few animals to use tools. It feeds largely on crabs and shellfish and often uses rocks to break open the hard shells.

### THREATS

Sea otters used to be hunted for their splendid fur and were almost wiped out by the beginning of the twentieth century. Since then they have been protected, but numbers are still low. Now the sea otter has other problems including pollution such as oil spills, which damage the animal's fur. It is also affected by the development of coasts in its range and by the fishing industry, as animals get trapped in nets. Now that numbers of Steller sea lions are low, orcas are preying more on sea otters.

## •IN THE FIELD•

Efforts are underway to increase the numbers of otters and mink. The Monterey Bay Aquarium in California is carrying out lots of research on sea otters to find out why numbers are increasing so slowly and what issues have the worst effects. They are also breeding from captive animals in order to return sea otters to the wild.

A sea otter breaks open a sea urchin on a rock.

# EUROPEAN MINK

**Scientific name:** Mustela lutreola
**Order/Family:** Carnivora/Mustelidae
**Range:** Eastern Europe and parts of Spain and France
**Size:** Head and body: up to 17 in. long; tail: 7 in.
**Conservation status:** Endangered

The mink always lives near fresh water and is semi-aquatic. It has a very dense coat, which is water repellent, and with its partly webbed feet it is a good swimmer. Mink usually shelter in dens in a riverbank or lakeshore during the day and come out at night to hunt for food. They eat a wide range of prey, including small mammals, birds, frogs, shellfish, fish, and insects.

## THREATS

The mink is one of the most endangered animals in Europe. It used to be hunted for its fur, although it is not as prized as that of the American mink. Now it is protected but it has suffered from the disturbance of its habitat and water pollution. It also faces competition for food from the larger American mink that have escaped from fur farms and are now found in the wild.

Giant Brazilian otters approach a caiman on the riverbank.

# GIANT BRAZILIAN OTTER

**Scientific name:** Pteronura brasiliensis
**Order/Family:** Carnivora/Mustelidae
**Range:** Northern South America
**Size:** Head and body: 4 ft. 6 in. long; tail: up to 3 ft. 3 in.
**Conservation status:** Endangered

Rivers, swamps, and lakes are home to this animal, the largest of the otters. It is a strong swimmer, using its webbed feet and powerful tail to push itself through the water as it hunts for prey such as fish, caimans, snakes, and birds. It lives in family groups of a mated pair and their young.

## THREATS

Like the sea otter, this otter used to be hunted for its fur and animals are still taken illegally. But now the main problems are water pollution, overfishing, and the destruction of large areas of its rainforest home.

# ANTELOPE, CAMELS, AND HIPPOS

These animals all belong to a big group of land mammals, which also includes cattle, sheep, and deer. The group name is Artiodactyla, which means even-toed. All these animals walk on hooves made up of two toes.

## BACTRIAN CAMEL

**Scientific name:** Camelus ferus
**Order/Family:** Artiodactyla/Camelidae
**Range:** China and Mongolia: Gobi Desert
**Size:** Head and body: up to 11 ft.; tail: 21 in.
**Conservation status:** Critically endangered

There are plenty of domesticated camels but probably only about 1,000 wild Bactrians remain. These camels live in the Gobi Desert, which has a very harsh climate, but they are able to tolerate extreme cold as well as heat and drought. The two humps are fat stores, which the animal can use for energy when food is in short supply. Bactrian camels will eat almost any plant they can find in their desert home.

### THREATS

Despite the fact that numbers of Bactrian camels are very low, some are still shot by hunters for food. They also have to compete with domestic animals, including camels, for grazing land. Wild camels are protected within the Great Gobi Reserve in Mongolia, but even this area is due to be disrupted by pipeline laying and mining for minerals.

### •IN THE FIELD•

The Wild Camel Protection Foundation has started a captive breeding program for Bactrian camels. The reintroduction of the Arabian oryx into the wild has been a success. When the population had begun to get very low in the 1960s an organization called Fauna and Flora International took some wild oryx to a zoo in Arizona where a captive breeding program was started. Animals were first released in Oman and Saudi Arabia in the 1980s and herds have been built up. But even these are at risk from poachers and some have been stolen for private collections.

The oryx is well suited to desert life. Its white coat reflects the sun's heat and its broad, splayed hooves help it walk on sand. Both male and female have impressive horns that are up to 27 in. long. Oryx live in herds of up to 30 animals. They feed on grass and other plants and often travel miles in search of food. They can live for long periods without drinking water, surviving on the water in their food.

### THREATS

For centuries, oryx were hunted by the Bedouin people for meat and hides but they took only what they needed and herds were large. In the twentieth century when sport hunters were equipped with guns and searched for their prey in trucks, far too many animals were killed and the Arabian oryx became extinct in 1972. Thanks to the captive breeding program, oryx have now been brought back to the area.

# ARABIAN ORYX

**Scientific name:** Oryx leucoryx
**Order/Family:** Artiodactyla/Bovidae
**Range:** Arabian Peninsula
**Size:** Head and body: 5 ft. 4 in.; tail: up to 23 in.
**Conservation status:** Endangered

# PYGMY HIPPOPOTAMUS

**Scientific name:** Hexaprotodon liberiensis
**Order/Family:** Artiodactyla/Hippopotamidae
**Range:** West Africa: Guinea to Cote d'Ivoire
**Size:** Head and body: up to 5 ft. 9 in. long; tail: 8 in.
**Conservation status:** Endangered

This hippo is rarely seen. It usually spends its days sleeping and wallowing in swamps or muddy rivers deep in the rainforest. At night it wakes up to feed on leaves and roots as well as fallen fruit. It generally lives alone, except for mothers with young.

### THREATS

Much of its forest home has been destroyed for logging or farming and pygmy hippos now live only in scattered areas. They are protected by law but are still killed for bushmeat. Reserves such as the Sapo Forest in Liberia and the Tai National Park in Cote d'Ivoire are vital if the pygmy hippo is to be saved from extinction. They breed well in captivity so the species can be kept alive that way.

# RHINOS, ZEBRAS, AND TAPIRS

All these animals are in the "odd-toed" group of hoofed mammals. Rhinos and tapirs have three toes on each foot. Horses and zebras have hooves made up of just one toe.

## GREVY'S ZEBRA

**Scientific name:** Equus grevyi
**Order/Family:** Perissodactyla/Equidae
**Range:** Ethiopia, Kenya
**Size:** Head and body: up to 10 ft. long; tail: up to 23 in.
**Conservation status:** Endangered

This splendid animal is the largest of the horse family. Like its relatives, it has a long neck, strong body, and slender legs. Its stripes are narrower than those of the plains zebra and it even has a stripy mane. It lives in dry grasslands and feeds on grasses as well as some leaves and shrubs. No one knows quite why zebras have stripes. It may be to help protect them from predators—it is harder for the predator to discern the outline of the zebra's body. But some experts think that the stripes are to do with zebra's social behavior, helping animals to identify each other and stay in touch.

### THREATS

Zebras have lost much of their grassland home to agriculture, and domestic livestock compete with them for grazing. Zebra skin was very fashionable for a while in the 1970s and many animals were killed for their hide. This trade is now illegal and there is far less poaching.

Grevy's zebra in the Lewa Reserve, Kenya.

With its big folds of heavy grayish skin, this animal looks like it is wearing a badly fitting suit of armor. Both males and females have a large horn, which can be up to 21 in. long. The horn is made of keratin (like our fingernails), not bone. The rhino feeds mainly on grasses, which it crops with the help of its strong upper lip. It also eats leaves, fruit, and branches. Despite its bulk it can run at speeds of 25 mph and is a good swimmer.

# GREAT INDIAN RHINOCEROS

**Scientific name:** Rhinoceros unicornis
**Order/Family:** Perissodactyla/Rhinocerotidae
**Range:** Northeast India, Nepal
**Size:** Head and body: up to 12 ft. 6 in. long; tail: 31 in.
**Conservation status:** Endangered

### THREATS
Much of the rhino's habitat has been cleared for farming and teak plantations. Large numbers of rhinoceros were once hunted for sport and for their horns which are used in traditional medicine. Although the rhinoceros is now protected, it is still killed illegally for its horn, which has fetched a higher price than gold on the black market.

## •IN THE FIELD•
The Indian rhino was once widespread across northern India but at the beginning of the twentieth century it was nearly extinct, with fewer than 200 animals in the wild. Conservation measures and strict protection—by armed guards in some areas —have gradually allowed numbers to increase to about 2,000 at present. There are plans to increase the number of reserves and sanctuaries and to involve more local people in the rhino's protection.

# BAIRD'S TAPIR

**Scientific name:** Tapirus bairdii
**Order/Family:** Perissodactyla/Tapiridae
**Range:** Central America; western South America: Colombia and Ecuador
**Size:** Head and body: up to 6 ft. 6 in. long; tail: 5 in.
**Conservation status:** Endangered

Baird's tapir lives in dense rainforest and is one of the largest mammals in Central America. It has a stocky body and short legs but is surprisingly nimble and good at clambering up hilly areas. It also likes water and often swims and wallows in rivers. The tapir feeds on leaves, fruit, and seeds. It has a long nose, rather like an elephant's trunk.

### THREATS
Rainforest has been cleared for cattle ranching and farming, and tapirs have suffered from this. They are now protected but are preyed on by jaguars and mountain lions and still killed by human hunters. Tapirs reproduce slowly—females have one young every three years—and it takes a long time for numbers to build up.

# ELEPHANTS

Elephants are the largest of all land animals and can live for 70 years or more. In 1970 there were probably about 1.3 million elephants. Less than 20 years later there were 600,000.

The African elephant is the world's biggest land mammal. Males are much larger than females and can stand up to 13 ft. high at the shoulder. The elephant has a huge body and thick, pillarlike legs. Its long trunk is used for smelling, breathing, and feeding. The trunk is immensely strong but the elephant also uses it gently to caress its young or companions. Both male and female African elephants have tusks, which are actually huge teeth. They are used for fighting, digging, and other tasks such as stripping bark off trees.

Elephants feed on plant material such as grass, leaves, twigs, bark, and fruit. Related females and their young live in family groups led by an old female. The bonds between them are very strong. Males leave the herd when they reach puberty and form groups with other males.

## AFRICAN ELEPHANT

**Scientific name:** Loxodonta africana
**Order/Family:** Proboscidea/Elephantidae
**Range:** Africa, south of the Sahara
**Size:** Head and body: up to 24 ft. 6 in.; weight: up to 8 tons (male)
**Conservation status:** Vulnerable

## THREATS

For centuries elephants have been killed for their ivory tusks, but in the twentieth century demand became particularly high and elephant numbers dropped sharply. Trade in ivory has been banned since 1990 but poaching still continues in some areas. Humans and elephants come into conflict as elephants can damage farmland crops while they search for food.

# ASIAN ELEPHANT

**Scientific name:** Elephas maximus
**Order/Family:** Proboscidea/Elephantidae
**Range:** India, Sri Lanka, Southeast Asia
**Size:** Head and body: up to 21 ft.; weight: up to 6 tons (male)
**Conservation status:** Endangered

The Asian elephant is smaller and lighter than African elephants and has smaller ears and a more rounded back. Only some males have tusks; females are tuskless. At the end of the trunk is only one fingerlike projection—the African elephant has two. Like African elephants, female Asian elephants live in groups with their young. Females give birth to one young after a pregnancy of about 22 months. On average the newborn baby weighs about 200 lb. All the females in the group care for the young and it can suckle from any of them. Asian elephants have a long history of being trained for work and they are still used to help clear timber in dense forest.

### THREATS

Hunting and loss of habitat as large areas are cleared for farming and to accommodate the rising human population have reduced the number of Asian elephants. Suitable habitat is now very fragmented and there are plans to create wildlife corridors to link protected reserves. There are often problems when elephants come into contact with people on farmland, leading to loss of both human and elephant lives. Elephants are protected by law but poaching of males for their ivory tusks still continues.

Elephant tusks confiscated from poachers.

### •IN THE FIELD•

In 1997, the ban on ivory trading was lifted to allow a limited trade between three African countries and Japan. But the Save the Elephant organization believes that the ivory trade is the greatest threat to the elephant's survival and that there should be a total ban once more.
All conservation organizations recognize the problems of elephants coexisting with people, often in areas where there is a desperate need for farmland and food. They are working to reduce the problems and make sure there are sufficient protected areas where elephants can live without disrupting agricultural land.

# RODENTS AND RABBITS

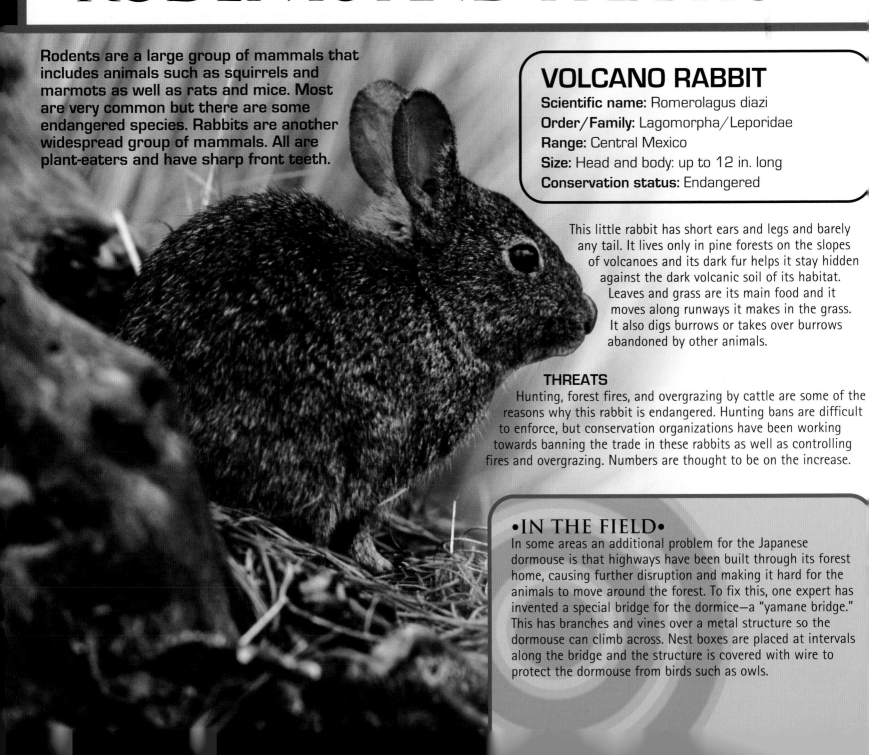

Rodents are a large group of mammals that includes animals such as squirrels and marmots as well as rats and mice. Most are very common but there are some endangered species. Rabbits are another widespread group of mammals. All are plant-eaters and have sharp front teeth.

## VOLCANO RABBIT

**Scientific name:** Romerolagus diazi
**Order/Family:** Lagomorpha/Leporidae
**Range:** Central Mexico
**Size:** Head and body: up to 12 in. long
**Conservation status:** Endangered

This little rabbit has short ears and legs and barely any tail. It lives only in pine forests on the slopes of volcanoes and its dark fur helps it stay hidden against the dark volcanic soil of its habitat. Leaves and grass are its main food and it moves along runways it makes in the grass. It also digs burrows or takes over burrows abandoned by other animals.

### THREATS

Hunting, forest fires, and overgrazing by cattle are some of the reasons why this rabbit is endangered. Hunting bans are difficult to enforce, but conservation organizations have been working towards banning the trade in these rabbits as well as controlling fires and overgrazing. Numbers are thought to be on the increase.

### •IN THE FIELD•

In some areas an additional problem for the Japanese dormouse is that highways have been built through its forest home, causing further disruption and making it hard for the animals to move around the forest. To fix this, one expert has invented a special bridge for the dormice—a "yamane bridge." This has branches and vines over a metal structure so the dormouse can climb across. Nest boxes are placed at intervals along the bridge and the structure is covered with wire to protect the dormouse from birds such as owls.

# MEXICAN PRAIRIE DOG

**Scientific name:** Cynomys mexicanus
**Order/Family:** Rodentia/Sciuridae
**Range:** Mexico
**Size:** Head and body: 12 in. long; tail: 3 in.
**Conservation status:** Endangered

The prairie dog is actually a kind of squirrel, with short legs and a small tail. It is a very sociable animal and lives in large family groups, which shelter in burrows. While the family feeds on grasses and other plants during the day, one prairie dog often acts as a lookout. If it spots danger, it shouts out an alarm call so the other animals can scurry back to the safety of their burrow. Females have a litter of about four young once a year.

## THREATS
Open plains are the preferred home of the prairie dog and much of this type of land is needed for farming and livestock grazing. Although this species is protected by law in Mexico, many animals have been poisoned as farmers consider them agricultural pests. An area has now been set aside where prairie dogs can live in safety and research is going on as to how best to balance the needs of farmers and these rare animals.

# JAPANESE DORMOUSE

**Scientific name:** Glirulus japonicus
**Order/Family:** Rodentia/Myoxidae
**Range:** Japan: Honshu, Shikoku, and Kyushu islands
**Size:** Head and body: up to 3 in. long; tail: 2 in.
**Conservation status:** Endangered

With its thick, soft fur and bushy tail, this little dormouse is an attractive animal. It lives in mountain forests and spends most of its time in trees—its Japanese name "yamane" means tree mouse—and it is an excellent climber. During the day it sleeps in a round nest made of lichen and bark, but at night it comes out to find food such as seeds, fruit, insects, and eggs. During winter it hibernates in a tree hollow or a bird box.

## THREATS
The main problem for the Japanese dormouse has been the loss of its forest habitat. The species is now strictly protected and there is a museum and study center for the dormouse. It is also one of the animals selected for special protection by the EDGE of Existence program. EDGE stands for Evolutionarily Distinct and Globally Endangered and aims to protect some of the most weird and wonderful of Earth's creatures.

# BATS

Bats are the only mammals that truly fly—creatures such as flying lemurs only glide through the air. Bats have wings made of skin, supported by the extra long fingers on the front limbs, and are extremely acrobatic in flight. There are about 1,000 species of bat worldwide.

## GHOST BAT

**Scientific name:** Macroderma gigas
**Order/Family:** Chiroptera/Megadermatidae
**Range:** Australia
**Size:** Head and body: up to 5 in. long; wingspan: 24
**Conservation status:** Vulnerable

This large bat gets its name from its pale, ghostly appearance when in flight. Like all bats it is active at night. During the day it roosts hanging upside down in caves, mines, or among rocks. It feeds on large insects as well as animals such as birds, frogs, small mammals, and even other bats, which it kills with its strong jaws.

## •IN THE FIELD•

The Rodrigues fruit bat has been a success story for the Jersey Zoo. In 1976 bats were taken to Jersey to start a captive breeding program. This has been so successful that Jersey has sent bats to other zoos and a captive colony has been started in Mauritius. For the species to survive in the wild, protection measures must be continued and the local population involved in the bats' recovery.

## THREATS

The ghost bat's main problems come from the disturbance of its roosting sites, either because of mining or quarrying activities or from tourists exploring caves. It has also faced competition for prey from foxes and cats introduced into Australia. Many of the areas where this bat lives are protected, and there is now a captive breeding program.

# RODRIGUES FRUIT BAT

**Scientific name:** Pteropus rodricensis
**Order/Family:** Chiroptera/Pteropodidae
**Range:** Mauritius: Rodrigues Island
**Size:** Head and body: up to 8 in. long; wingspan: 30 in.
**Conservation status:** Critically endangered

Not long ago this bat was almost extinct, but conservation efforts seem to be succeeding and the population is rising once again. The Rodrigues fruit bat lives in mangrove swamps and rainforest and roosts in caves or trees during the day. At dusk it flies out to feed on insects and fruit, which it finds with its sharp eyes and good sense of smell. It doesn't use echolocation. These bats live in large colonies and females give birth hanging upside down. The young bats cling on to their mothers at first but can hang by themselves at only two weeks old.

**THREATS**
Loss of its forest home—and with it food and roost sites—has been the main problem for this bat. It also used to be hunted for food, and hunting may have driven the bat to extinction in Mauritius where it used to be found. Cyclones are common in this area and bats are blown out to sea where they cannot survive. Captive breeding and protection of the forest are helping the bat population to recover.

# BECHSTEIN'S BAT

**Scientific name:** Myotis bechsteini
**Order/Family:** Chiroptera/Vespertilionidae
**Range:** Scattered areas of Europe
**Size:** Head and body: 2 in. long; wingspan: 12 in.
**Conservation status:** Vulnerable

This was once the most common British bat, but it is thought that only around 1,500 remain in the UK. Bechstein's bat lives in woodland and roosts in trees or bat boxes during the day. At night it hunts insects such as moths and beetles by echolocation: the bat makes high-pitched sounds that bounce off anything in their path and uses these echoes to find its prey and navigate.

**THREATS**
Large areas of woodland where these bats lived have been destroyed but it is not clear what else has affected the species. The population is now monitored in Britain and bat boxes are being put in areas where the bats live. The bat is now protected under English Nature's Species Recovery Program.

The marsupial group of mammals includes possums, wallabies, and wombats, as well as kangaroos. Most marsupials live in Australia. Females have a pouch on the front of the body where their young finish their development.

## LEADBEATER'S POSSUM

**Scientific name:** Gymnobelideus leadbeateri
**Order/Family:** Diprotodontia/Petauridae
**Range:** Southeast Australia
**Size:** Head and body: up to 6 in. long; tail 7 in.
**Conservation status:** Endangered

With its big eyes, bushy tail, and soft striped coat this little possum is an attractive creature. It has very particular habitat requirements—it can live only in mixed ash forests where there are enough old trees with hollows for use as nests. During the day this possum shelters in its tree nest, then comes out at night to feed on insects and spiders, which it finds under bark. It also eats gum from the acacia or wattle tree. Animals live in pairs with their young but the female is dominant and she defends her territory against other females. The female has a small pouch. Her newborn young crawls to the pouch and stays there for 85 days until it is big enough to start moving around and feeding by itself.

### THREATS
The possum's main problem is its very specific nesting needs, as many of the old ash trees it likes to nest in are cut down for timber or burned in fires.

### •IN THE FIELD•
Leadbeater's possum was thought to be extinct after terrible fires destroyed large areas of forest in 1939, but in 1961 it was rediscovered. Conservationists have been working to increase the population with plans for a protected reserve. They are also experimenting with providing nest boxes for the animals to use instead of tree hollows. To protect the few remaining northern hairy-nosed wombats, a national park has been established in Queensland and wombats are also being bred in captivity.

# GOODFELLOW'S TREE KANGAROO

**Scientific name:** Dendrolagus goodfellowi
**Order/Family:** Diprotodontia/Macropodidae
**Range:** Indonesia, New Guinea
**Size:** Head and body: up to 30 in. long; tail 33 in.
**Conservation status:** Endangered

Tree kangaroos are good climbers and look quite different from ground-living kangaroos. With their short back legs and strong arms they are well adapted for life in the trees. The long tail helps the tree kangaroo balance as it leaps from branch to branch. It is generally active at night when it feeds on leaves, fruit, grass, and flowers. Like other kangaroos, the female has a pouch into which her tiny young climbs soon after its birth. It remains there for up to a year, feeding on her milk and growing.

## THREATS
This kangaroo has been hunted for its meat and is now rare. Much of its forest habitat has also been destroyed and there are reasonable numbers of these animals only in national parks, protected areas, and reserves.

A female Goodfellow's tree kangaroo with a young peeking out of her pouch.

# NORTHERN HAIRY-NOSED WOMBAT

**Scientific name:** Lasiorhinus krefftii
**Order/Family:** Diprotodontia/Vombatidae
**Range:** Queensland, Australia
**Size:** Head and body: up to 3 ft. 3 in. long; tail: 2 in.
**Conservation status:** Critically endangered

This shy, generally nocturnal creature is now extremely rare. It has a stocky body, short legs, and large front paws with strong claws for digging. The female is slightly bigger than the male. These wombats live in dry, sandy grassland or acacia woodland where they dig burrows with a number of tunnels and chambers. They shelter in the burrow during the day and at night feed mostly on grasses. Surprisingly, this wombat can run at up to 25 mph if it needs to escape from danger. The female has a pouch with a rear-facing opening.

## THREATS
Competition with livestock for grassland grazing has been a problem for this wombat as has the disruption of its habitat by farming and land clearance. Wombats are also preyed on by dingoes.

# PARROTS

There are more than 300 different kinds of parrots, including macaws, lovebirds, cockatoos, and lorikeets. Most live in tropical areas.

## HYACINTH MACAW

**Scientific name:** Anodorhynchus hyacinthinus
**Order/Family:** Psittaciformes/Psittacidae
**Range:** Brazil, Bolivia, Paraguay
**Size:** Up to 3 ft. 3 in. long
**Conservation status:** Endangered

The largest parrot in the world, the hyacinth macaw has bright blue feathers, yellow face markings, and a very long tail. It lives mostly on the hard fruit of a few kinds of palm trees, such as the acuri, which it can break open with its powerful hooked beak. The macaw nests in tree hollows or on cliffs. The male brings food to the female while she incubates her eggs and the young stay with their parents for up to six months.

### THREATS

For this bird, its beauty has been its problem. In the 1980s thousands were captured for the pet trade, leaving the hyacinth macaw on the edge of extinction. Birds were also hunted locally for food and for their feathers. The fact that the macaw has a limited diet and prefers to make its nest in a specific kind of tree make it particularly vulnerable to habitat disturbance and destruction. Trade in these birds is now strictly illegal, but some poaching does go on as the birds can be sold for large sums of money. Thanks to a WWF project in the Pantanal area of Brazil, numbers are on the increase and there are hopes to expand the work to other areas to save the species.

A hyacinth macaw feeding on palm tree fruits.

# KAKAPO

**Scientific name:** Strigops habroptila
**Order/Family:** Psittaciformes/Psittacidae
**Range:** New Zealand: offshore islands
**Size:** Up to 24 in. long
**Conservation status:** Critically endangered

The kakapo is the heaviest of all parrots and the world's only flightless parrot. It uses its wings to help balance as it runs along on the ground but cannot fly. And unlike other parrots it is active at night— its name means "night parrot." The kakapo lives alone and feeds on plant material such as roots, seeds, leaves, and flowers. It breeds only every two to five years.

## THREATS
The kakapo is now extinct on mainland New Zealand. The first settlers used to kill the birds for meat and for their beautiful green feathers, but the birds' problems really began when European settlers arrived in the nineteenth century. They brought animals such as dogs, cats, and stoats, which preyed on the kakapo and their eggs. Being flightless, it was hard for the kakapo to escape. Introduced deer also ate much of the kakapo's food.

# YELLOW-CRESTED COCKATOO

**Scientific name:** Cacatua sulphurea
**Order/Family:** Psittaciformes/Psittacidae
**Range:** Indonesia
**Size:** Up to 13 in. long
**Conservation status:** Critically endangered

This beautiful cockatoo has white feathers and a golden-yellow crest. It lives in forest and on agricultural land and feeds mainly on seeds, berries, and nuts. A sociable bird, it often gathers in large groups and the birds keep in touch with loud screeching calls.

## THREATS
The main reason for this bird's decline is the pet trade, but cockatoos are now bred in captivity for sale as pets to stop the demand for wild birds.

## •IN THE FIELD•
The only surviving kakapo have been taken to islands off the coasts of New Zealand where there are no predators. The birds are very carefully monitored and chicks are hand-reared to make sure they survive. In 2008 the population of birds had risen to 92, showing the success of the recovery program. The aim is now to find a larger island which can be cleared of predators and where more kakapo can live, and ultimately to bring kakapo back to mainland New Zealand.

# EAGLES AND VULTURES

Eagles, hawks, and falcons are all birds of prey and have strong claws and beaks for killing and eating their food. Vultures are meat eaters too but they feed on carrion—animals that are already dead.

## PHILIPPINE EAGLE

**Scientific name:** Pithecophaga jefferyi
**Order/Family:** Falconiformes/Accipitridae
**Range:** Philippines
**Size:** Up to 36 in. long; wingspan: up to 6 ft. 6 in.
**Conservation status:** Critically endangered

This magnificent bird is the world's largest eagle. A powerful hunter, it has a sharply hooked beak for tearing its prey apart, strong legs, and feet tipped with big curved claws. It is also known as the monkey-eating eagle because it hunts monkeys, as well as flying lemurs, squirrels, bats, and birds, in its rainforest home. The female bird lays only one egg at a time and the parents care for their young until it is around 17 or 18 months old.

### THREATS
Like all rainforest creatures, this eagle has suffered badly from logging and the destruction of the forest for development. It has also been hunted in the past although it is now protected by law.

### •IN THE FIELD•
The Philippine Eagle Foundation has now opened a center for the protection and conservation of this species and has had some success with breeding birds in captivity. They also work to encourage eagle-friendly practises in mining and logging and to involve local people in their work with the eagles.

# CALIFORNIA CONDOR

**Scientific name:** Gymnogyps californianus
**Order/Family:** Falconiformes/Cathartidae
**Range:** Western North America
**Size:** Up to 53 in. long; wingspan: up to 9 ft.
**Conservation status:** Critically endangered

The California condor is the largest flying bird in North America—and one of the rarest birds in the world. A member of the New World vulture family, this huge bird soars for miles on its long, broad wings as it searches for carrion. It has excellent eyesight and can spot food, such as dead cattle, sheep, rabbits, or deer, from high above the ground. The condor nests on a cliff ledge and lays a single egg. The young stays with its parents for up to a year so condors can only breed every other year.

## THREATS

The California condor became rare because of hunting, the collection of its eggs and the reduction in its food supply as large mammals became less common in North America. Many also died from lead poisoning after eating animals killed with lead shot. By 1981 there were only 22 birds in the wild and in 1987 the last eight were captured and a breeding program started. Birds have now been reintroduced into the wild in California, Arizona, and Mexico, but some are still killed by lead poisoning and collisions with electric power lines.

# INDIAN VULTURE

**Scientific name:** Gyps indicus
**Order/Family:** Falconiformes/Accipitridae
**Range:** India and Pakistan
**Size:** Up to 36 in. long; wingspan: up to 7 ft. 4 in.
**Conservation status:** Critically endangered

Like other vultures, this bird has a strong hooked beak and a featherless head and neck. It feeds on carrion and is often seen with other vultures, such as the white-rumped vulture. They do an important job—if dead animals are left to rot they are a health hazard. The vultures often nest in groups on cliffs or in trees. They make huge nests of sticks and leaves in which the female lays just one egg.

## THREATS

These vultures used to be common but in recent years they, and other vultures, have suffered a dramatic decline. Experts were puzzled at first but they have discovered that the problem is caused by a drug called diclofenac used on cattle. The drug causes kidney failure in vultures when they eat animals that have been given this drug. Conservation organizations recommend banning the drug and breeding birds in captivity to help restore the wild population.

# PENGUINS AND OTHER SEABIRDS

Some seabirds spend their lives soaring over the ocean while others are excellent swimmers and find their food in the sea. All are at risk from ocean pollution.

## YELLOW-EYED PENGUIN

**Scientific name:** Megadyptes antipodes
**Order/Family:** Sphenisciformes/Spheniscidae
**Range:** New Zealand
**Size:** Up to 27 in. long
**Conservation status:** Endangered

This is one of the most endangered of all penguins. Its Maori name is "hoiho" which means "noise shouter" and it does indeed have a shrill call. Its most distinctive features are its yellow eyes and the yellow marking that runs across the eyes and around to the back of the head. Like all penguins, this bird cannot fly but uses its wings like flippers when in the water. It is an excellent swimmer and diver and spends much of its time at sea hunting fish and squid. Less social than most penguins, it does not gather in huge groups but usually lives in pairs, which mate for life. It nests in forest or scrub where there is some cover.

### THREATS
Introduced predators, such as ferrets, stoats, and cats, have caused problems for the penguins as they eat eggs and kill young birds. There may also have been food shortages in some areas because of rising sea temperatures, and some of the forest nesting areas have been destroyed or disturbed. Penguins also get trapped in fishing nets. The Yellow-eyed Penguin Trust was set up to protect this bird and learn more about the reasons for its rarity. They have arranged for the fencing in of some breeding areas so birds and their nests aren't disturbed by cattle. They are also working toward the conservation of coastal forest nesting areas and controlling predators within these areas.

### •IN THE FIELD•
One tactic to protect seabirds that is being promoted by the Save the Albatross campaign is the use of bird-scaring devices to keep birds away from fishing lines. These work just like scarecrows on farmland: a curtain of colored plastic streamers is attached to a rope over the fishing area to scare birds away. The campaigners are working with fishermen to encourage the use of these devices.

# BLACK-FOOTED ALBATROSS

**Scientific name:** Phoebastria nigripes
**Order/Family:** Procellariiformes/Diomedeidae
**Range:** Northern Pacific Ocean
**Size:** Up to 32 in. long; wingspan: up to 7 ft.
**Conservation status:** Endangered

Although one of the smaller albatross, this is still a very large seabird. It glides for hours over the ocean on its long wings, swooping down to feed on fish, squid, and shellfish or scavenge scraps or fish waste thrown from boats. Pairs mate for life and breed on beaches or bare slopes on the Hawaiian Islands or islands off Japan.

## THREATS

Numbers of these birds are declining fast. Thousands of birds every year are caught in fishing nets or on long line hooks as they search for food and they can't breed fast enough to make up these losses. Pollution, such as oil spills, is also a problem and many birds choke when they accidentally swallow plastic waste. Hawaiian breeding beaches are now part of the National Wildlife Refuge scheme but more work needs to be done to encourage fishermen to safeguard these birds.

Also known as the flightless cormorant, this bird has very small wings and cannot fly. Instead it swims and dives in shallow water to find prey such as fish and octopus, using its strong legs and webbed feet to push itself through the water. The cormorant's feathers aren't waterproof and after a fishing expedition it is often seen on the shore with its wings held out to dry.

# GALÁPAGOS CORMORANT

**Scientific name:** Phalacrocorax harrisi
**Order/Family:** Pelecaniformes/Phalacrocoracidae
**Range:** Galápagos Islands
**Size:** Up to 3 ft. 3 in. long
**Conservation status:** Endangered

## THREATS

As it cannot fly and doesn't tend to move far from its home range, this bird is very vulnerable to disturbance from humans or other animals, and to pollution such as oil spills. Birds are also caught in fishing nets. All live within the Galápagos National Park and there are plans to monitor the population more closely and ban fishing with nets in its range.

# CRANES AND CRANELIKE BIRDS

Cranes are large, long-legged birds that wade in shallow water to find prey. Related to cranes are a range of other birds such as rails and bustards.

## GREAT BUSTARD

**Scientific name:** Otis tarda
**Order/Family:** Gruiformes/Otididae
**Range:** Scattered areas of Europe and Asia
**Size:** Up to 3 ft. 3 in. long; wingspan: up to 8 ft. 3 in. (male)
**Conservation status:** Vulnerable

Male great bustards can be up to twice the size of females and at up to 44 lb may be the heaviest of all flying birds. Bustards usually live on grassland or open farmland where they feed on leaves and seeds as well as insects and small animals such as lizards and voles. At the start of the breeding season males gather in groups to perform a mating display for the females. This is called "lekking." The males fluff out their feathers and puff up their throat pouches to make themselves look more impressive.

### THREATS

Great bustards are protected now but large numbers were hunted in the past. Much of their habitat has also been changed to intensive farming land or disrupted by the building of roads and other structures. Pesticides and fertilizers have affected the birds and they are still hunted in China and Ukraine. Conservation projects are working to establish protected areas for these birds and to release captive-reared birds in areas where numbers are declining or already low.

A male great bustard performing his courtship displa

# TAKAHE

**Scientific name:** Porphyrio hochstetteri
**Order/Family:** Gruiformes/Rallidae
**Range:** New Zealand
**Size:** Up to 25 in. long
**Conservation status:** Endangered

Thought to be extinct until rediscovered in the Murchison mountains on New Zealand's South Island in 1948, the takahe has glossy plumage, a heavy red beak, and bright red legs. It cannot fly but flaps its wings in courtship displays. It feeds on grasses and seeds but catches invertebrates when it has hungry chicks to feed.

## THREATS

A flightless bird, the takahe is particularly vulnerable to disturbance and to introduced predators such as stoats, which attack ground nests and eat eggs and young. Introduced deer also compete with the takahe for grass. A takahe reserve has now been set up in Fiordland National Park and birds have been taken to offshore islands where there are no predators.

## •IN THE FIELD•

Great bustards were once common in Britain but were hunted to extinction by the middle of the nineteenth century. The Great Bustard Group is aiming to reestablish these birds in the UK. Since 2004 chicks reared in Russia have been brought to the UK and, after a quarantine period, released into the wild. It is hoped that these birds will start to breed.

A whooping crane with its young.

# WHOOPING CRANE

**Scientific name:** Grus americana
**Order/Family:** Gruiformes/Gruidae
**Range:** North America
**Size:** Up to 5 ft. long; wingspan: 7 ft. 6 in.
**Conservation status:** Endangered

Most whooping cranes migrate between Canada, where they breed in marshland in summer, and salt marshes in the southern United States, where they overwinter. They catch small prey, such as shellfish, insects, frogs, and fish, and also eat some plants. At the start of the breeding season the birds perform spectacular dancing displays. The nest is usually made of plants and rushes and the female lays two eggs.

## THREATS

Once found all over North America, whooping cranes were hunted for food and sport, and their eggs stolen by collectors. In 1941 only 16 birds remained. Numbers have been built up again with the help of captive-bred birds, but the species is still at risk. Much of the cranes' wetland habitat has been disrupted and many die after colliding with power lines.

# CASSOWARY, KIWIS, AND GEESE

These birds are all from different families, but they are all now suffering from similar problems. They are very vulnerable to introduce predators against which they have few defenses.

## SOUTHERN CASSOWARY

**Scientific name:** Casuarius casuarius
**Order/Family:** Struthioniformes/Casuariidae
**Range:** New Guinea; Australia: Queensland
**Size:** Up to 5 ft. 6 in. tall
**Conservation status:** Vulnerable

Cassowaries are large, flightless birds related to emus. They have strong legs and feet, and the inner toe of each foot bears a long sharp claw. If attacked, the cassowary kicks out with its clawed feet and can cause serious injury. Generally, though, it is a peaceful creature and lives in the rainforest feeding on fruit. The female lays her eggs on the groun where they are incubated by the male bird. Once the chicks hatch he protects them until they are more than a year old.

### THREATS
Cassowaries have lost at least half of their rainforest habitat in recent years. Birds are also killed by traffic and disturbed by dogs. Wild pigs are another problem—the pigs trample on nests and eggs and compete with the birds for food.

### •IN THE FIELD•
Conservationists have discovered that the protection of the cassowary is important for the rainforest as a whole. The birds feed on fruit and many of the seeds pass straight through them, undigested. As the birds move around the forest they spread the seeds of the fruits they eat and many plants depend on this for their survival. Experts are concerned that if the cassowary disappears so will many plants and, in turn, other animals that depend on those plants. The natural world is finely balanced and the loss of one element can have terrible consequences.

# GREAT SPOTTED KIWI

**Scientific name:** Apteryx haastii
**Order/Family:** Struthioniformes/Apterygidae
**Range:** New Zealand: South Island
**Size:** Up to 20 in. long
**Conservation status:** Vulnerable

This is the largest of the five species of kiwi and, like the others, it cannot fly. It evolved at a time when there were no mammals in New Zealand and food was plentiful on the ground so it had no need of flight. The kiwi is one of the few birds with a good sense of smell and it has nostrils at the end of its long beak. It feeds by probing the ground with its beak, sniffing out prey such as insects, spiders, worms, and other small creatures. It also eats some fallen fruit and leaves. The female lays just one enormous egg each spring.

## THREATS

The kiwi is the national symbol of New Zealand. The most important reason for the kiwi's decline is the introduction of predatory mammals to New Zealand. Stoats, cats, dogs, and possum prey on adults and young and eat kiwi eggs. Kiwis are radio-tracked to protect them from predators. Researchers discovered that more than 90 percent of chicks died before six months so now some eggs are removed, hatched, and reared in captivity until they can fend for themselves.

# HAWAIIAN GOOSE

**Scientific name:** Branta sandvicensis
**Order/Family:** Anseriformes/Anatidae
**Range:** Hawaiian Islands
**Size:** Up to 27 in. long
**Conservation status:** Vulnerable

Also known by its Hawaiian name "nene," this goose is the national bird of Hawaii. It is smaller than most geese and has longer legs, enabling it to run over rough ground with ease. It feeds on grass and fruits. Females lay their eggs on the ground. Young goslings cannot fly until they are three months old so are at great risk from predators.

## THREATS

These birds were almost extinct at the beginning of the twentieth century. Many were hunted for food and their eggs stolen, and they have also suffered from introduced predators such as the Indian mongoose and dogs. The population has now risen, but this is mainly thanks to captive-bred birds being released every year and the species still needs protection. Many of these geese are killed crossing roads, and in areas where they live there are road signs saying "nene crossing" to urge drivers to take extra care.

# SONGBIRDS

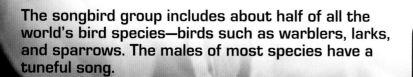

The songbird group includes about half of all the world's bird species—birds such as warblers, larks, and sparrows. The males of most species have a tuneful song.

## BLACK-CAPPED VIREO

**Scientific name:** Vireo atricapilla
**Order/Family:** Passeriformes/Vireonidae
**Range:** Southern United States; northern Mexico
**Size:** Up to 4 in. long
**Conservation status:** Vulnerable

A lively bird, this vireo lives among dense, scrubby vegetation where it picks insects and spiders off leaves. Males and females are similar in size but the female has a grayish, not black, cap on her head. Birds nest in the southern United States in the summer, then migrate to northern Mexico where they spend the winter.

### THREATS

The conversion of its scrubby habitat to farmland and urban areas has affected this bird and reduced its population significantly. But another serious problem has been the increase in numbers of brown-headed cowbirds. Instead of making their own nests, the cowbirds lay their eggs in other birds' nests—including those of the vireo. The cowbird chicks are bigger and stronger than the vireos so they get most of the food and many vireo young die. In Texas there is now a protected area where cowbirds have been removed and the vireos can breed in peace. Vireo numbers are going up and there are plans for other such areas.

## •IN THE FIELD•

Trade in animals as well as feathers, skins and other items is monitored and controlled by an organization called CITES—the Convention on International Trade in Endangered Species. Its purpose is to make sure that any form of trade does not endanger an animal's survival. There are different levels of protection according to how endangered an animal is. For some, limited trade is allowed, while for others it is banned entirely.

Larger and more spectacular than most songbirds, birds of paradise are among the most beautiful of all birds. Males have brightly colored, decorative feathers that they use in displays to attract females, which have plainer plumage. The male has bright blue feathers on his body, wings, and tail, and some extra-long tail streamers. In his display he hangs upside down to show off his feathers to full effect. These birds live in tropical rainforest and feed on fruit.

# BLUE BIRD OF PARADISE

**Scientific name:** Paradisaea rudolphi
**Order/Family:** Passeriformes/Paradisaeidae
**Range:** Papua New Guinea
**Size:** Up to 12 in. long, plus tail streamers
**Conservation status:** Vulnerable

## THREATS

Rainforest is disappearing in New Guinea as the population increases, and this affects the birds of paradise. They have been hunted for their colorful feathers but are now protected by law and trade in feathers is restricted. Research continues to find out more about these birds' needs. One idea is to promote their value as a flagship species to boost ecotourism to the country.

# CERULEAN WARBLER

**Scientific name:** Dendroica cerulea
**Order/Family:** Passeriformes/Parulidae
**Range:** United States, Central America, northern South America
**Size:** Up to 4 in. long
**Conservation status:** Vulnerable

This little warbler is rarely seen as it spends most of its time high in the trees, but you may hear its trilling call. The male has much brighter blue feathers than the female, which is blue-green. Insects are its main food but it does eat some plants in winter. Most birds migrate between the northern United States where they breed in summer, and winter feeding areas in northern South America.

## THREATS

Once common in some areas, warbler populations have declined rapidly, largely due to loss of habitat as forest is cleared for building.
In South America native trees are replaced by coffee and coca plants. The Cerulean Warbler Atlas Project is studying the birds in different areas to determine what they need to survive. There are plans to create protected areas of forest where these birds, and other species, can flourish.

# TURTLES, TORTOISES, AND CROCODILES

These animals are all reptiles. Turtles live in rivers and oceans while their tortoise relatives live on land. Gavials belong to the crocodile family.

## •IN THE FIELD•

Marine turtles and their eggs are now protected in most places. Turtle Excluding Devices can be attached to shrimp nets to avoid accidental capture and longline fishing is banned in a large area of the northern Pacific at certain times of year. Conservationists at Galápagos National Park collect and hatch eggs and keep the young in captivity until they can defend themselves from dogs and other animals.

## LEATHERBACK

**Scientific name:** Dermochelys coriacea
**Order/Family:** Testudines/Dermochelyidae
**Range:** All oceans
**Size:** Up to 5 ft. 3 in. long; weight: up to 1,300 lb
**Conservation status:** Critically endangered

The leatherback is the world's largest turtle. It gets its name from its flexible shell, which is covered with a layer of leathery skin. Seven ridges run the length of the shell. Jellyfish are the leatherback's main food and it can dive as deep as 3,000 ft. in search of prey. It is a strong swimmer and migrates thousands of miles between feeding areas in temperate seas and breeding beaches in tropical zones. After mating the female drags herself up onto a beach where she digs a pit in the sand. She then lays around 100 eggs, covers them up, and returns to the sea. When the eggs hatch, the baby turtles make their own way to the water.

## THREATS

In the last 10 years populations of the leatherback have been reduced by 80 percent in some parts of its range. Some are accidentally caught in fishing nests; others die after swallowing plastic bags or garbage they mistake for jellyfish. Some beaches traditionally visited by the turtles have been disturbed or built on, and many eggs are taken from their sand nests by poachers.

# GALÁPAGOS GIANT TORTOISE

**Scientific name:** Geochelone nigra
**Order/Family:** Testudines/Testudinidae
**Range:** Galápagos Islands
**Size:** Up to 5 ft. 6 in. long; weight: about 550 lb.
**Conservation status:** Vulnerable

This huge tortoise may have given the Galápagos Islands their name—galápago means tortoise in Spanish. The world's largest tortoise, it is also one of the longest-lived of all vertebrate animals and there are animals of well over 100 years old. It spends most of its day feeding on plants including cacti. Like all land tortoises, it can pull its head and legs into its shell when attacked. The female lays up to 16 eggs, which she buries in a hole in the ground.

## THREATS

Thousands of tortoises were captured by sailors in past centuries and taken on board as a supply of fresh meat. Now they are protected, but poaching continues. Today's threats are from animals introduced into the Galápagos such as rats, dogs, and pigs. They eat eggs and young, while goats and cattle eat the plant life.

# GHARIAL

**Scientific name:** Gavialis gangeticus
**Order/Family:** Crocodylia/Gavialidae
**Range:** Rivers in Bangladesh, India, Nepal, and Pakistan
**Size:** Up to 19 ft. 6 in. long
**Conservation status:** Critically endangered

The gharial has a long, narrow snout, lined with small, sharp teeth—ideal for catching fish, the gharial's main prey. Young gharials feed mostly on insects. The gharial spends most of its life in water and doesn't move as easily on land as some other crocodiles. In the breeding season the female hauls herself on to the riverbank where she digs a pit and lays around 40 eggs.

## THREATS

The gharial was nearly extinct 30 years ago but protection measures and captive breeding saved the species. Numbers are low again, partly due to the disruption of rivers by dams. Prey can be scarce; gharials are poached by fishermen and eggs taken for use in traditional medicine. Stronger conservation measures are clearly needed if this animal is to survive.

# SNAKES AND LIZARDS

**Snakes and lizards all belong to the same group of reptiles—the squamates. Several hundred of these are now increasingly rare.**

The Komodo dragon is the world's largest lizard. It is certainly an awesome sight with its heavy body, strong tail, and flickering forked tongue. A fierce predator, this lizard hunts animals such as deer and wild pigs, but it will also eat any carrion (animals that are already dead) that it comes across. It can move with surprising speed and has been known to attack and kill humans. Females lay eggs which they bury in the ground and leave to incubate and hatch by themselves. Young dragons spend much of their first year in trees catching insects to eat—on the ground they are vulnerable to predators, including other komodo dragons.

## KOMODO DRAGON

**Scientific name:** Varanus komodoensis
**Order/Family:** Squamata/Varanidae
**Range:** Indonesia: Komodo, Rinca, and Flores islands
**Size:** Up to 10 ft. long
**Conservation status:** Vulnerable

### THREATS

Numbers of these extraordinary reptiles are going down. One problem has been the loss of prey species, such as deer, through hunting. The dragon is probably extinct on the island of Padar for this reason. The animals are now officially protected but they are sometimes killed by locals to protect livestock.

The komodo uses its sensitive tongue to help it find prey.

### •IN THE FIELD•

Tourism can be a problem for animals but it could help save the Komodo dragon. Thousands of people visit Komodo and the other islands each year in the hope of seeing one of these creatures and the income from tourism encourages local people to safeguard the dragons.

# GIANT GARTER SNAKE

**Scientific name:** Thamnophis gigas
**Order/Family:** Squamata/Colubridae
**Range:** Western United States
**Size:** Up to 63 in. long
**Conservation status:** Vulnerable

This is one of the largest garter snakes. Its color varies from brownish to olive-green, with light-colored stripes running down its back. This snake lives in and around water and needs a home with grasses or bulrushes at the water's edge where it can bask in safety. Fish, frogs, and tadpoles are its main foods. During the winter, this snake spends most of its time in a burrow left by a mammal.

## THREATS

Loss of habitat and water pollution are problematic for the giant garter snake as many waterways have been disrupted by building and land clearance. Many snakes have now started to live in rice fields in California and in managed wildlife reserves. Giant garter snakes are now protected in areas such as the Golden Gate National Recreation Area, but more research is needed if the species is to be saved.

# FIJI BANDED IGUANA

**Scientific name:** Brachylophus fasciatus
**Order/Family:** Squamata/Iguanidae
**Range:** Fiji, Tonga; introduced to Vanuatu
**Size:** Up to 31 in. long
**Conservation status:** Endangered

This handsome, bright green iguana lives in forests and is a good climber. Its long tail helps it balance as it leaps among the branches. Leaves, fruit, and flowers are its main food but it also eats some insects and invertebrates. Only the males have the distinctive broad stripes across the body that give them their common name. Females are green all over, sometimes with some lighter spots down their sides.

## THREATS

Some of this iguana's forest habitat has been destroyed but the biggest threat has been from the mongooses and cats introduced to the islands. They prey on the iguanas and eat their eggs and young. The iguana is now protected by law and the population has been helped by a captive breeding program at the Fear-No-More Zoo on the island of Naitauba in Fiji. The zoo's aim is to preserve and protect Fiji's wildlife.

# FROGS AND TOADS

Frogs and toads are amphibians. Most breed in water but are equally at home on land, where they can hop, jump, and even climb trees. More than one in three species of amphibian is now rare and threatened with extinction.

## GOLDEN FROG

**Scientific name:** Atelopus zeteki
**Order/Family:** Anura/Bufonidae
**Range:** Central America: Panama
**Size:** Up to 2 1/2 in. long
**Conservation status:** Critically endangered

This brilliantly colored frog has a slender body, long legs, and smooth skin. It lives in forested areas near streams, and males defend their territory and attract mates by hand-waving signals. Like most frogs, they breed in water. The female lays a string of eggs with a jellylike coating for protection, and these hatch into tiny swimming tadpoles. The tadpoles develop legs and grow into miniature versions of their parents, able to move on land.

### THREATS

Now extremely rare, the golden frog has become a national symbol for wildlife conservation in Panama. The most serious problem for this frog, and many others, has been a disease caused by the chytrid fungus. This damages the frog's skin and can cause suffocation—frogs breathe partly through their skin. The golden frog has also suffered from habitat loss, chemicals poisoning streams, and the over-collection of animals for the pet trade.

# YOSEMITE TOAD

**Scientific name:** Bufo canorus
**Order/Family:** Anura/Bufonidae
**Range:** California
**Size:** Up to 2 1/2 in. long
**Conservation status:** Endangered

Like most toads, this species has a stocky body and warty skin. Males are generally greenish in color with only a few dark markings or none at all. Females are light colored with lots of dark blotchy markings. These toads live in damp meadows or forest edges and breed in shallow pools. They are usually active during the day and the male makes a particularly tuneful call— the Latin name "canorus" means tuneful. These toads feed on insects and other small invertebrates.

## THREATS

This toad has disappeared from much of its range and numbers have gone down, even in protected areas such as Yosemite National Park. Reasons include fungus disease, pollution from farm chemicals, and poisoning from windborne pesticides. The toad is also affected by increasing numbers of cattle, which trample down the grasses it shelters among and disrupt the habitat.

# GREEN AND GOLD FROG

**Scientific name:** Litoria raniformis
**Order/Family:** Anura/Hylidae
**Range:** Southeast Australia and Tasmania; introduced in New Zealand
**Size:** Up to 4 in. long
**Conservation status:** Endangered

This frog is also known as the growling grass frog because of its deep croaking call. It belongs to the tree frog family and is a good climber, but spends much of its time on the ground and in ponds and streams.

## THREATS

This frog has lost much of its habitat as ponds are drained and rivers polluted. The species is protected and in Tasmania farmers leave plants alongside rivers and ponds to provide cover. In 2000 a site for the Olympic Games tennis courts at Homebush Bay, Sydney, was found to be a habitat of these frogs. Work was stopped and the building moved elsewhere.

# FISH

Fish were the first vertebrate animals to live on Earth. There are two main groups of fish—bony fish, which have a skeleton made of bone, and sharks and rays which have skeletons of cartilage. Many kinds of fish, both sea and freshwater, are now rare due to overfishing and pollution.

## SOUTHERN BLUEFIN TUNA

**Scientific name:** Thunnus maccoyii
**Order/Family:** Perciformes/Scombridae
**Range:** South Atlantic, South Pacific, Indian Ocean
**Size:** Up to 14 ft. long
**Conservation status:** Critically endangered

One of the largest bony fish, this tuna has a sleek, streamlined body and a crescent-shaped tail. It generally swims at around 2 mph but can speed through the water at more than 40 mph. It generally gathers in shoals that are constantly on the move in the open ocean, searching for prey such as other fish, squid, and octopus. They can dive down to 1,600 ft. or more.

### THREATS

This tuna is now rare because of overfishing. Its flesh has a very high fat content, making it particularly popular in Japan for sashimi. There have been attempts to reduce the numbers taken, but much stricter protection will be needed for the species to survive. This fish is now reared in fish farms off the coast of Australia and it is hoped that this will reduce pressure on the wild population.

## •IN THE FIELD•

The United States has been the biggest market for beluga caviar but has now banned imports from wild fish—farmed caviar is still allowed. This will reduce illegal poaching and may give the fish a chance to recover. Beluga live a long time—up to 100 years—but do not start breeding until they are 15 to 18 years old, so it could take many years for numbers to build up again.

A southern bluefin tuna caught in a fishing net

## THREATS

The hammerhead is often caught for its fins, which are used in shark fin soup, but is also caught accidentally with other species. There are no protection measures for this species at present but there are plans to ban the taking of this shark for its fins alone.

# GREAT HAMMERHEAD SHARK

**Scientific name:** Sphyrna mokarran
**Order/Family:** Carchariniformes/Sphyrnidae
**Range:** Warm, temperate, and tropical waters in all oceans and in Black and Mediterranean seas
**Size:** Up to 20 ft. long
**Conservation status:** Endangered

As its name suggests, this huge shark has a hammer-shaped head, with one eye at each end. There are many theories why the head is shaped like this. It may be that the large surface area increases the shark's sensory abilities or allows a greater area for electro-receptors—the shark hunts by detecting the electric field around prey. The hammerhead generally swims in coastal waters and preys on many different kinds of fish, squid, and shellfish. It also seems to be particularly fond of stingrays, despite their poisonous barbs.

# BELUGA

**Scientific name:** Huso huso
**Order/Family:** Acipenseriformes/Acipenseridae
**Range:** Black and Caspian seas and in rivers in Europe
**Size:** Up to 10 ft. long
**Conservation status:** Endangered

Also known as the great sturgeon, the beluga is the largest freshwater fish in Europe. It hunts smaller fish on the seabed with the help of the sensory whiskerlike barbels around its mouth. Every two to four years, mature adults travel up into rivers where they mate. A female may lay several million eggs at a time which attach themselves to stones on the riverbed. After hatching, the young fish swim back downstream to the sea.

## THREATS

Overfishing is the main threat to the beluga, and its eggs are also gathered and eaten as caviar—beluga caviar is the most expensive kind. Also, much of the beluga's habitat has been affected by pollution and the building of dams. Beluga numbers have gone down more than 90 percent in the last 20 years.

# INSECTS AND SPIDERS

There are at least a million known insect species in the world, more than any other type of creature, and many more yet to be discovered and named. Spiders are not insects—they belong to a separate group called arachnids. There are at least 35,000 known species of spider.

## APOLLO BUTTERFLY

**Scientific name:** Parnassius apollo
**Order/Family:** Lepidoptera/Papilionidae
**Range:** Europe and Central Asia
**Size:** Wingspan: up to 3 ¼ in.
**Conservation status:** Vulnerable

A large butterfly with black and orange-red markings on its wings, the apollo usually lives in mountain meadows. Its caterpillars are black with red spots on their sides and their main food plant is stonecrop (sedum). When full-grown, the apollo caterpillar makes a cocoon on the ground. About a week later the butterfly emerges.

### THREATS

Loss of habitat and over-collection have been the main threats for this butterfly. It has also been affected by pollution, and caterpillars have faced competition from other animals for their food plants. Trade and collection of this butterfly are now restricted and butterflies are being bred in captivity to try and boost the wild population.

### •IN THE FIELD•

The caves where the Kauai cave wolf spider lives are on private land, but the U.S. Fish and Wildlife Service is working with the landowners to preserve the habitat and monitor the spider. Gates have been installed to prevent human disturbance, and plant life is being restored.